An Unsung American Hero

by Sasha Griffin

HOUGHTON MIFFLIN HARCOURT
School Publishers

PHOTOGRAPHY CREDITS: **Cover** (c) © Massachusetts Historical Society, Boston, MA, USA/The Bridgeman Art Library, (b) Siede Preis. **Title page** © The Granger Collection, New York. **2** (t) © Massachusetts Historical Society, Boston, MA, USA/The Bridgeman Art Library. (b) Siede Preis. **3** © The Granger Collection, New York. **5** © The Granger Collection, New York. **6** © Bettmann/CORBIS. **7** © North Wind Picture Archives. **9** © Getty Images. **10** © The Granger Collection, New York. **12** © The Art Archive/Culver Pictures/Picture Desk. **13** PhotoDisc/Getty Images. **14** © The Granger Collection, New York. **15** Painting by Don Troiani www.historicalimagebank.com. **16** Courtesy of the Council, National Army Museum, London, UK/The Bridgeman Art Library. **17** PhotoDisc/Getty Images.

Printed in China

ISBN-13: 978-0-547-01762-4
ISBN-10: 0-547-01762-6

13 14 15 16 0940 19 18 17 16
4500569761

An American Hero

When you think of the American Revolution, you may remember important battles, or heroes like George Washington and Paul Revere. Yet there are stories behind the battles, and heroes who are not as well known.

Joseph Warren is one of those heroes. Although he did fight in some battles, his work off the battlefield was much more important. A well-respected doctor, Warren became a political writer and speaker. He worked tirelessly as an organizer and Patriot leader.

Warren's persuasive articles and speeches and his political work for the Patriot cause helped bring about the American Revolution.

Early Years

Joseph Warren was born in Roxbury, Massachusetts, in 1741. His parents were farmers, so Joseph grew up climbing apple trees and playing in the fields. Sometimes he would go to Boston to sell milk from his family's cows. He must have been proud of the new strain of apple his father developed. The apple, named for his father, was called the "Warren russet."

But one day, a terrible tragedy struck the Warren family. Joseph's father fell off a ladder while gathering apples in the orchard. The fall broke his neck, killing him. Fourteen-year-old Joseph was now the man of the family. When he was not at college, it was up to him to do some of the harder work around the farm.

Joseph Warren grew up in Roxbury, Massachusetts. Roxbury is now a neighborhood in Boston.

The year his father died was also Joseph's first year at Harvard College. A story from these days shows that Joseph was a fearless young man. As the story goes, some friends locked him out of their dormitory room as a prank. Joseph climbed onto the roof and then lowered himself down an old drain pipe. When he reached his open window, he climbed through. Just then, the drain pipe pulled away and crashed to the ground. Joseph would have fallen with it had he been a minute too slow! Calmly, Joseph looked down and stated, simply, that the pipe had done its job.

This courage would later be seen in many parts of Joseph Warren's life.

A Colonial Doctor

After graduating from college, Warren became a doctor. Around that time, an epidemic of the dreaded smallpox disease broke out in Boston. Dr. Joseph Warren worked tirelessly, treating smallpox patients at a special hospital. He lived in the hospital for several months, tending to the needs of hundreds of suffering patients.

When the epidemic was over, Dr. Warren was well known throughout Boston. He had a reputation for being gentle, charming, and sensitive. In 1764, Warren married Elizabeth Hooton, a wealthy and beautiful young woman.

Dr. Warren may have worked in a hospital much like this.

Patients came to Dr. Warren from all walks of life. One of his patients was a carpenter named William Dawes. Warren would later send Dawes and Paul Revere to warn the colonists that the British army was approaching. Other patients included John and Abigail Adams, John Hancock, and even the colony's governor, Thomas Hutchinson.

Many of Dr. Warren's patients paid him with items such as flour, blankets, buckles, and shoes. Others paid him with money. By 1769, Dr. Warren had become a very successful and sought-after physician. So when he entered politics, it was not because he thought he could make a better living, but because he had very strong feelings about what was happening to the colonists at that time.

Entering Politics

In the 1760s, the British Parliament passed a series of laws. These laws gave Britain more control over the colonies. One law was the Stamp Act. The taxes raised from the Stamp Act would help pay for the British troops and officials stationed in the colonies.

Warren was outraged by the Stamp Act. He believed that officials paid with this tax money would not represent the people fairly. Why couldn't the colonists elect their own officials? Why couldn't they collect and spend their own tax money as they saw fit?

These strong feelings led Joseph Warren to write letters and newspaper articles. In his writing, he deliberately used

Colonial Government

Although they were British subjects, American colonists had grown used to governing themselves. Voters elected representatives who made laws and passed taxes. But the governor, who was appointed by the British king, could overturn these laws whenever he wished.

words that would appeal to people's emotions. Warren's writing was very persuasive, and many people agreed with him. "No taxation without representation" became the colonists' slogan. Riots broke out. Merchants refused to import British goods. Representatives from nine of the colonies met. They declared that Parliament could not tax the colonies because the colonies had no representatives in Parliament.

Colonists had to pay for stamps like these. The stamps were put on official documents, newspapers, playing cards, and paper.

Finally Britain repealed the Stamp Act. But soon, the British Parliament replaced it with new laws and taxes that angered the colonists even more.

Over the next few years, Warren became one of the most important Patriot leaders. His newspaper articles and letters often portrayed British officials as foes of the colonists. Warren's writing was full of strong emotional appeals. He wanted to convince his readers to agree with him. Then they would convince their representatives to work toward freedom from taxation without representation.

Warren was an important member of many political groups. He gained the respect of many legendary leaders of the time, including Samuel Adams and Paul Revere.

A "Horrid Massacre" in Boston

Tensions grew between the colonists and British officials. Street fights between Boston townspeople and British troops broke out. Warren may even have helped plan some of the actions against the British.

On the evening of March 5, 1770, a crowd of angry colonists surrounded a British guard. More soldiers arrived to support him. The townspeople shouted insults and threw snowballs and oyster shells at the soldiers. One of the soldiers shot into the crowd. The fight grew, and more shots were fired. British troops poured into the street like water gushing from a pump. When the colonists finally retreated, three men lay dead in the snow. Two more would soon die from their wounds.

The colonists held a town meeting. They selected Warren to join a committee to talk with British officials. The British knew that Warren had a lot of influence with the colonists. They worried that he might encourage people to become violent. When they met, Warren and the committee got the British to agree to remove their troops.

A week later, Warren and two other men wrote about what happened on March 5. They called the event a "horrid massacre." Warren hoped to turn public opinion against the British even more. And in fact, the Boston Massacre did begin to turn people's thoughts toward the possibility of revolution.

The Boston Massacre fanned the flames of American resistance to British rule.

More Taxes and Tea

Warren's influence continued to grow. Although he didn't have a position in the government, he had a big part in Boston politics. He not only wrote but also made speeches. He and Paul Revere helped organize a political group for Boston's craftsmen and laborers.

As a member of the Committee of Correspondence, Warren wrote letters to other towns and colonies warning them to protect their rights. Through all this, he continued his medical practice. He was still the most popular and well-known doctor in Boston.

In 1773, Parliament passed the Tea Act to get the colonists to pay taxes on tea. Warren and other Patriot leaders wanted people to stop buying tea to protest the taxes. Tea was extremely popular at the time, so they worried that people would buy their favorite drink, no matter what.

Colonists expressed their opinions and made decisions in town meetings.

Warren led an angry crowd to the tea merchants' warehouse. The crowd demanded that the merchants refuse to sell their tea when it arrived. The merchants, not wanting to agree to Warren's plans, locked themselves in the warehouse. Then the mob of townspeople took the doors off their hinges. They threatened the merchants, who still would not agree to stop selling tea. The crowd held the merchants in the warehouse for more than an hour. Warren's role in this event was considered high treason in England. Although he was a hero to the colonists, the British saw him as a traitor.

When a shipment of tea arrived, Warren tried to return it to England. British officials would not allow this. Warren worked with Samuel Adams to unite the colonists. Warren wrote letters inviting people from nearby towns to attend a meeting. There, he and several others spoke about the importance of resisting British taxes. They convinced the group to prevent the unloading and sale of the tea. Everyone agreed to a plan of action, even though they knew it would be dangerous.

On the evening of December 16, a number of colonists disguised themselves as Indians. They boarded several ships and dumped 342 chests of tea into the harbor. This became known as the Boston Tea Party.

No one knows for certain whether Warren was on the ships that night. Yet he was considered one of the main leaders of the Boston Tea Party. Some British officials wanted to arrest and try Warren for treason. If he were convicted of being a traitor, he would be hanged. But the British knew that a jury of colonists would never convict their hero. Instead, the British passed new laws to punish all of Massachusetts.

Bostonians continued to oppose the Tea Act. At a second "Tea Party" early in 1774, a group of men forced a tea merchant to leave town during a snowstorm.

War!

For the next year or so, Warren worked tirelessly to oppose unjust British laws. When the British closed the port of Boston, Warren helped create jobs for unemployed workers. He collected and distributed donations to the poor. His speeches inspired many people, and some of the documents he wrote were adopted by the Continental Congress, the first independent government of colonial America. Warren organized a provincial congress to govern Massachusetts. When he became a member of this congress, it was the first official government job he had held.

The colonies moved closer to war with Britain. Warren made sure there were weapons and other supplies for when the fighting began. He also wisely gave instructions to all colonists to hide the ammunition from the British.

On April 18, 1775, Warren learned that British troops would begin marching toward Concord. He believed that they would try to capture two important Patriot leaders, Samuel Adams and John Hancock. He feared that the soldiers would also try to steal the colonists' supplies and ammunition.

The order to assemble troops for battle could normally only be made by a vote of the Committee of Safety. Warren was a member of this committee, but he was the only member in Boston that night. A decision had to be made quickly, and Warren made it.

He sent for Paul Revere and William Dawes. He told each man to ride to Concord by a different route. If one were captured, the other might still get through. The two men were to warn Adams and Hancock and alert the American militia that the British were coming. Warren's decision was a signal for war.

Paul Revere's legendary ride has been retold in books, films, and a famous poem by Henry Wadsworth Longfellow.

The Minutemen

The American militia was made up of common people like farmers, shopkeepers, and craftsmen. These volunteer soldiers often had no formal military training. Yet they were prepared to fight at a minute's notice. This is why they were often called "minutemen."

At dawn the next day, the Charles River was shimmering as Warren crossed it. He was headed toward the first battle of the Revolutionary War. He had heard that the British and Americans were already massed at Lexington, so he rode quickly in that direction. On the way, he came upon two British soldiers trying to steal an old man's horse. Warren drove the soldiers off and continued on. Unfortunately, he rode right into the rear of the British troops and was almost captured. Luckily, the soldiers didn't recognize him, so they let him go.

When Warren reached Lexington, he found the American soldiers disorganized and frightened. The Battle of Lexington was over, and the British had gone on to Concord. Warren rallied the minutemen and organized them so they would be ready to fight again. When the British began to retreat from Concord, the Americans had the advantage.

The Americans followed the British back toward Boston. The British outnumbered the Americans, but the colonial militia didn't give up. They shot at the lines of British soldiers from inside houses and from behind trees and fences. In one town, the militia fired at the enemy from both sides of the long main street. The British fought back. Men from both sides were killed and wounded, but Warren led his men on. He was in the middle of heavy gunfire when a musket ball barely missed his ear. It came so close that it knocked a hairpin from his hair.

Many Americans saw Warren as a magnificent hero. He wasn't a politician starting a war for others to fight. He was willing to fight for his beliefs. Although he continued to plan war strategy, Warren wanted to be an officer in the army. The Massachusetts Provincial Congress made him a major general on June 14, 1775.

The Battle of Lexington

At Bunker Hill

Three days later, on June 17, the British army attacked the American forces at the Battle of Bunker Hill. Warren attended a Council of War meeting to discuss the battle, but he was not satisfied with planning from a distance. Warren decided to walk through dangerous battlefields so he could join the American forces.

Bunker Hill Monument

Colonel William Prescott, the commander in the battle, was desperate for reinforcements. Many men had deserted. Others refused to join the battle because they would have to cross an area the British were bombarding, the same area that Warren had just crossed on foot.

When Warren arrived, Colonel Prescott asked him to leave because it was so dangerous. When Warren refused to leave, Prescott offered to let him command the American forces. Again, Warren refused, pointing on that Prescott was more experienced. Warren had come as a volunteer, not an officer.

The British were firing heavily upon the hill. Warren plunged into the battle, fighting beside his countrymen and treating those who were wounded.

Warren's bravery inspired the frightened men around him. As the British soldiers advanced, the Americans ran low on ammunition. In order not to waste what little they had, Colonel Prescott ordered, "Don't fire until you see the whites of their eyes."

Finally, there were only about 150 colonial soldiers left, including Warren. When they had no more ammunition, they threw rocks and used their guns like clubs. But this was no match for British bayonets. It was time for a retreat. Warren was one of the last to leave. As he made his way down the back of the hill, he was fatally shot.

Warren didn't live long enough to see America become an independent nation. Yet his passionate words and brave acts inspired many others to work and fight for independence. Joseph Warren, like George Washington and Paul Revere, is an American hero. And he is not forgotten. Today, every state in New England has a town named in his honor.

Responding

✓ **TARGET SKILL** **Conclusions and Generaliza-tions** What story details would lead a reader to conclude that Joseph Warren was brave? Copy and complete the chart below.

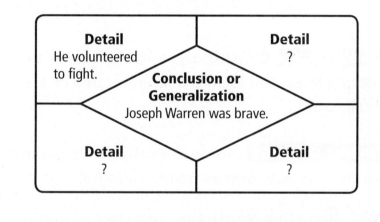

Detail
He volunteered to fight.

Detail
?

Conclusion or Generalization
Joseph Warren was brave.

Detail
?

Detail
?

Write About It

Text to Text *An Unsung Hero* tells about a leader who guided people through hard times. Think about someone you've read about who did the same. Write a few paragraphs explaining how that person led others.

✓ **TARGET SKILL** **Conclusions and Generalizations**
Use details to explain ideas that aren't stated or are
generally true.

✓ **TARGET STRATEGY** **Analyze/Evaluate** Think carefully
about the text and form an opinion about it.

GENRE **Narrative Nonfiction** gives factual information
by telling a true story.